PURPOSE

POEMS ABOUT LIVING
YOUR LIFE'S PURPOSE

DANA ZIMMERMAN

www.ThatGuysHouse.com

hey,

Welcome to this wonderful book brought to you by
That Guy's House Publishing.

At That Guy's House we believe in real and raw
wellness books that inspire the reader from a place of
authenticity and honesty.

This book has been carefully crafted by both the
author and publisher with the intention that it will
bring you a glimmer of hope, a rush of inspiration and
sensation of inner peace.

It is our hope that you thoroughly enjoy this book
and pass it onto friends who may also be in need of a
glimpse into their own magnificence.

Have a wonderful day.

Love,

Sean Patrick
That Guy.

Dedication

This book is dedicated to my family and friends. They are the one's who inspired me to write these poems. Each poem has a unique meaning to me and has helped me through the good and tough times. It is also dedicated to all those who need to hear these words, to help them through moments of good times, and moments of struggle. It has been a book to help me get through depression and my own anxieties in life. They have lifted me up and refocused my thoughts many times, which has allowed me to become the strong, bright person I am today.

welcome to your

PURPOSE

Let your Light Shine

Who says you need to step back and not take
care of you?
Don't allow those to tell you what to do.
Let your light shine
Let the sun be your sign
Take care of your mind, body and spirit
Create for yourself, no limits
The credit to allow yourself to be happy
This is where your spirit is free
Let your Light shine for all to see
Your aura is as bright as can be
Practice your affirmations to keep your goal clear
Show your gratitude for everything far and near.
Stay present in what is here in the moment
This is where you will have your enjoyment
Let your light shine bright
Keep it in plain sight

When Life is in the Fog

Looking too far in front of you
Will cause your mind to stew
Just like walking in the morning fog, keep your focus in
front of you
It clears your mind and you will know just what to do
As you come upon the fork in the road
In that moment you will do the bold
Take the path that is less traveled
Adventure awaits, the ones you have marveled
You see, being in the fog is quite the adventure
one can take
You to grow and limits will break
As the fog lifts and you can see the glorious sun
In your life you will see all the work done
Take a breath and take in your view
This breath you take, your life anew

I turn problems into learning opportunities, ones I can share with others and to grow

Tricks and Treasures

Life is full of tricks and treasures
Which one are you going to choose for measures?
Tricks can make your mind think you're crazy
It can make your emotions lazy
Allowing other's crap into your life
Will cause your emotions a lot of strife
Keep their issues at bay
You can only guide them along the way
It is up to them to choose
It shall not be you to lose
Treasures are living in your mindful space
Taking positive steps at a steady pace
Allowing you to be your authentic self
Will keep you in good emotional health
In every situation thrown your way
Find the treasure for abundance it will pay
Abundance in happiness
Abundance in pure bliss
Find that treasure that you long to cherish
At this point your self-love will not perish

OUR FRIENDS IN HEAVEN

So many lives lost in such little time
As you see life on earth can stop on a dime
One thing we should remember and cherish
Their souls will never perish
Even though we are selfish and want them to stay
They are in heaven looking our way
When we get sad wishing they were here
In our hearts they will always be near
Whatever pain that they endured
We know now that God has cured

Take the time to listen empathetically. It may mean the world to someone that they are heard

Living on the Edge

On the edge of time
My life stops on a dime
I reflect on my day
For the best possible way
As I look at the mountain
My heart flows like a fountain
As I walk along this winding trail
I grow wings in the winds I sail
High above in the trees
I soar around completely free
My mind is clear
My heart is pure
There is nothing that I fear
Back in time you shall know
The trail was rough I had to grow
There were fears and agreements I learned
These I eventually burned
Living on the edge to me
Is living life fully free

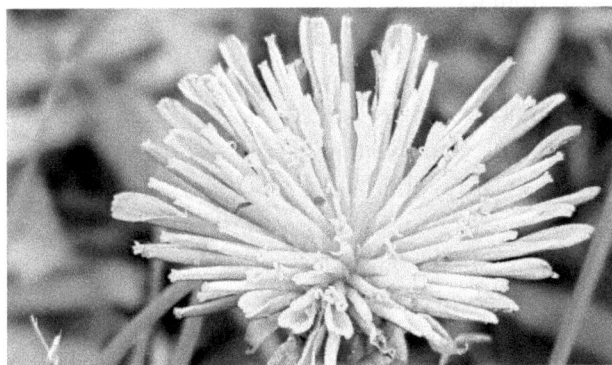

I choose to be who I am

No matter where I am
I will do what I want to do
Say what I want to say
And be who I want to be
No one can make that choice but me
You can choose what you want to do
You can choose what you want to say
You can choose what you want to be
Who says it's any different? The universe
calls out to you
Every life is a dream. You are living that
dream so create.
Because you can choose who you are.
I know, I choose to be who I am.

It's okay to have moments of sadness, it means you are normal

Day after Election

As we awake today with the news of the new president
I remind you to stay in your true work that you present
Hold the people in power and love
As this will then rise above
Take the time and meditate
This will open that shiny gate
The gate to passion of our great Country
Where it is the land of the free
Free of corporate and political corrupt
Free from prejudices that erupt
It is our heart that needs to move in action
To create this great Country's satisfaction
A place where people can call it home
A place for others to freely roam
Meditate with me as it is love we seek
To keep the love at its peak
The love will shine its light right through
Even with the new president's view

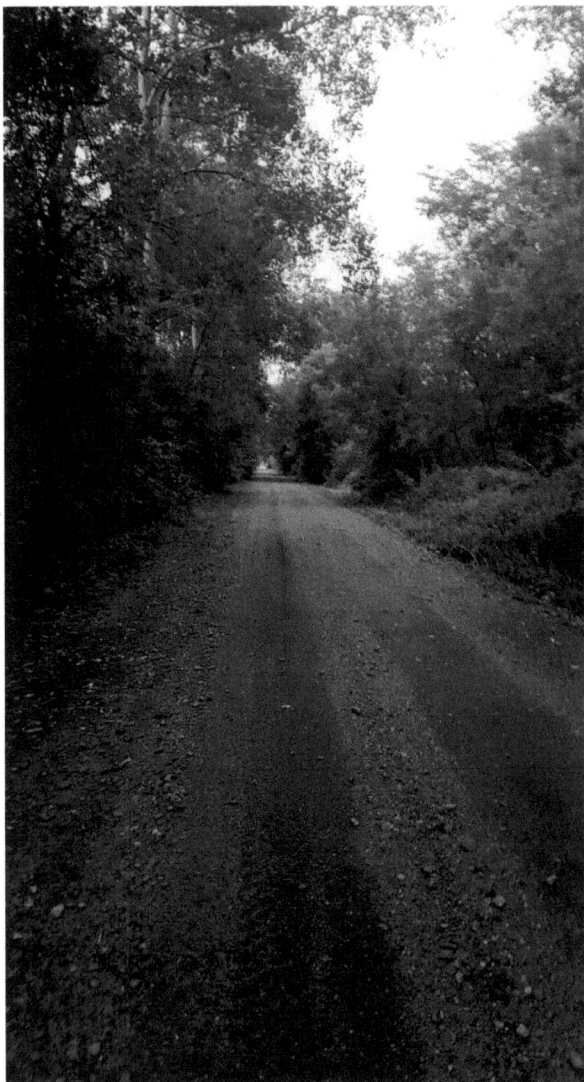

The Trail

Walking along the trail
I know I will not fail
I release what is inside me
So my soul can be free
I close my eyes and dream
Peace and calm are my team
Love is found everywhere
Anger and hate I do not dare
Happiness blooms like a flower
It's like cleansing your body in the shower
Walk along the trail with me
As all of this you will see

Affirmation of Empowerment:

I desire to be gentle and kind
A warrior of all emotions
A unique soul that will shine where ever she is
A person that shows love to all
A change agent in this world

Living in the Present

What is it like living in the present you ask?
Really, it is a very simple task.
Take a breath and breathe with me.
For this is all it take for you to see.
Listen to the birds sing in the tree
Listen to the water flowing free
Cam your mind and find your peace
Then you can create your masterpiece
In the present here and now
You can divorce your vows.

Letting Go

Look at this picture created anew
A place that is solemn and true
The sun is setting for the end of day
All your fears are swept away
Pick some stones and create your temple
Meditate and release your intention, very simple
Let go of what does not serve you
Let go of the day past to start anew
Lie down your head to sweet dreams
It is there, your path gleams
As you wake your day is bright
Peace is in plain sight.

Sometimes in life you just have to say "I am Awesome!"

A Special Friend is...

Hard to find
One of a kind
Will always care
Very Rare
Gives a shoulder to cry on
A positive ion
Never goes away
You are today
There with laughter
Forever after
You are to me
You will always be

An Emotional Crash

When souls are sad and your days are blue
What are some of the things you can do?
You can think of the gloom ahead in your days
Or you can find the good that is heading your way
You can crawl in a hole and hide from the world
Or you can allow bright colors in to be swirled
You can treat your body like an emotional
punching bag
Or run around the yard and play tag
You could wallow in sorrow with a bad look
Or you could curl up and read a great book
You could create destruction down the wrong path
Or run some water and take a hot bubble bath
Whatever it is that is making your soul sad or
your day blue
There are others around you that do love you
Don't take your life just because of one day
Because around the corner there are others that
want you to stay
There are dreams yet to be fulfilled and
laughter to be heard
Don't let just one day allow your judgment
to be blurred.

I am doing the best I can today with what I am taught.

Round Bale of Emotions

Like Hay, Intertwined into a bale
Our emotions are messy, they do not fail
As each emotion arises throughout the day
The round bale is harvested under the sun ray
As you unbind the bale to nourish the animals
Check with your emotions to ensure they are rational
Allow each emotion to flow through you and be
Just like the round bale sits there for those to see
Each straw of hay entangled with another
Each emotion intertwines as you rediscover
Rediscover yourself and be true to you
The round bale sits there to nourish the new
Take care of yourself and keep emotions in check
The next round bale is being made and placed on deck.

Time

Look upon the clock and the time will tell
That clock dictates our lives we live each day
Why are there only numbers one through twelve?
As the clock ticks our minds can go astray

Seconds, minutes, hours, days, months, years
our measurement
Our moments, memories, time together
Cherish for positive development
Measurements of time creates the pressure

But stress of knowing where or what to be
Creating that special moment that sticks
Anxiety will not release from me
Depression holds on to me with tight grips

Do not my friend, measure time by unit
Measure by memories sent in orbit

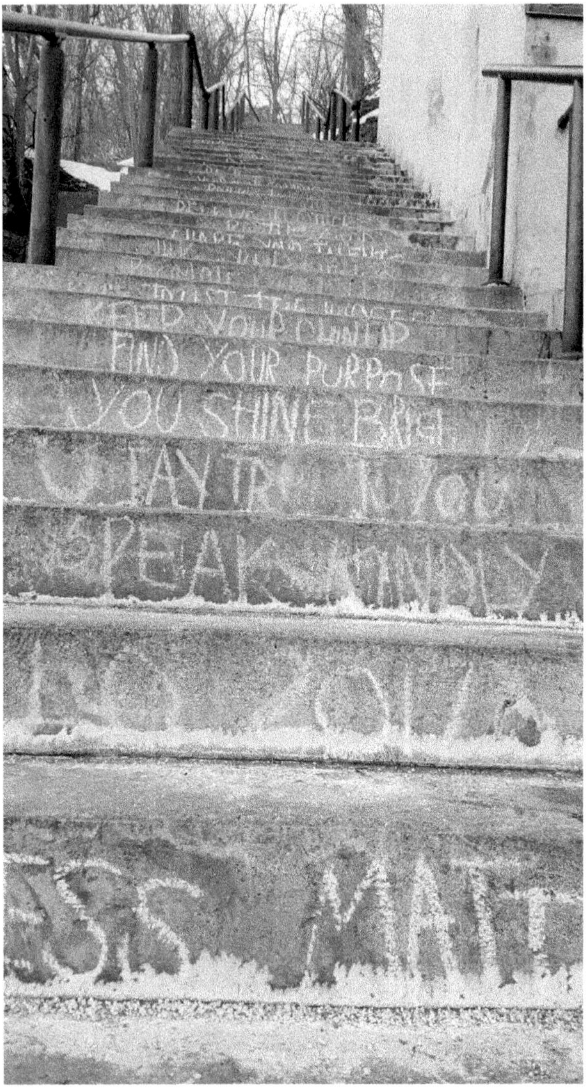
FIND YOUR PURPOSE
YOU SHINE
SPEAK

Gratitude Affirmation:

I am grateful for the day upon us
I am grateful for my family and friends
I am grateful for the teachers in life
I am grateful for my health
Thank you, Thank you Thank you

Open Doors

As the door opens, that has a rough look
Take a glance, it's your life awaiting
A new chapter of a book
Don't let other do the dictating
Create your life for that beautiful view
Happiness awaits you that is so true
Look around, there is so much to see
Colors are vibrant, do I need to plea?
A plea for you to see the present
Staying in the past will create discontent
Don't allow your thought to control your feeling
These thoughts will slow your healing
As you pass through the door that is open
Your life will be filled with good emotion
Emotion that you know all is good
It is somewhere that you can show your livelihood
As the door now behind you closes
A new one opens a new life it exposes

Shining Heart

Let your heart shine as bright as the big sun
Add some color just for fun
Hear the birds singing in the trees
Calming your mind as still as can be
See the blue sky that is never ending
Allowing the universe to do the mending
Smell the flowers to be in the moment
Observe the scene to keep yourself present

I am energy. The energy flows and heals others

End of Day

As the sun sets and the vortex opens
Your heart will sing and you will be filled
with emotions
Center yourself and clear your mind
Here is where answers to questions you find
Connect yourself with earth and sun
This is where true work is done
It's okay to be your authentic self
And keep your body in perfect health
Keep your intentions true to you
Don't let others dictate you
As the vortex closes and your head lays to rest
In your heart and soul you will feel life's zest.

BYOH (Be Your Own Hero)

At the end of the day who is it you need to save?
Yourself. Be a hero to yourself.
Sometimes the villain can play the devil's advocate,
But don't allow the villain to conquer all.
The villain can be negative self-talk and the myths you
tell yourself.
Be your own Hero I request this today.
Be your advocate. Keep false beliefs at bay
By being your own hero you can conquer the pain
You begin to see no limits and all the great work done.
Keep your chin up and the passion burning.
These super powers you are about to discover
Are far greater in power than the villain will
try to smother.
Stand tall and stand strong.
The storm is coming at you playing the sad song.
As that storm approaches
Use your superpower and your coaches
This team will pull you through the storm
And you will feel as if you are reborn

I am kind and compassionate to those around me

Friendship Walk

Like this tiny trail that disappears
Memories are made through the years
Looking at the sky above
My heart sings the song of a morning dove
The sky so blue, the clouds so white
Connect your soul with the bright white light
The pillars of rock stand firm in the ground
My heart is beating, hear that magical sound
Do you dare to follow that tiny trail
Secrets to life are ready to be unveiled
Come, walk along this trail with me
Together we will find the treasure's key
What is the treasure you may ask?
It will reveal with one simple task
Take the key to unlock the clue
The treasure is there looking at you
You will find it there in your friend
Walking together the love will transcend

My Spark is not igniting

My spark is not igniting
It is my heart that is truly fighting
I am curious of the path to come
Questions flood my mind and then some
Why am I so afraid to see the answer?
Because my fears are such a cancer
Rip open and through those fears today
Release your mind and your heart will play
It will play the beautiful song of your life
Your soul will not be stabbed with the knife
Reactions to your trigger, keep them in check
It can cause you to become an emotional wreck
Why is my spark not igniting today?
Please someone, show me the way

I am abundance: abundance of love, knowledge,
kindness,
and wisdom

Love is in the air, don't you see?

Love is in the air don't you see?
Signs all around you even in the tree.
Open your eyes and fill your space
Love will come at sonic pace.
Signs of love are everywhere.
Take the adventure if you dare
Do you see them like me?
I opened my eyes its love I see.
People hugging and lending a hand.
Oh how life can be so grand.
When your eyes are wide open taking in the view
Unlimited possibilities are endless for you

Give me a Reason

Give me a reason to love
It is light shining from above
Give me a reason to be a friend
They are with you to the end
Give me a reason to be alive
It is an adventure, take the drive
Give me a reason to be grateful
It takes more work to be hateful
Give me a reason to just be
There are no others like me
Why do you need a reason may I ask
There is no need to wear a mask
Live your life every day
Even when the skies are grey
The world is your playground
Go ahead and soar all around
My reason today for you my friend
Is to stop looking for reasons, they have no end.
Be you! Be Brave! Be Kind! Be Loving!
Your purpose will show like the river rushing!

Affirmation of Love:

I deserve to be loved the way I desire to be loved and respected. I am beautiful and vibrant in all aspects. My needs are met the way they need to be through loving touch and gestures. Love is a beautiful connection between two souls who are passionate about each other. My partner and I can communicate our needs openly, honestly, and lovingly. I am strong and set clear boundaries for myself.

Magical Moments

What are those moments that you remember?
Each person has their own moment in time
That create magic when you surrender
Where it seems like your life, stops on a dime
Magical moments are ones to treasure
They are created in life one by one
These are the moments that show kind gestures
Allow one to be created, have fun
When you surrender your mind to your heart
Your heart sings and your soul is glowing bright
That's when magic is flowing off the chart
Like fireworks shooting off in the night
Share with me your magic moment today
No two moments are created the same

My Body, My Temple

My body is my temple
This is just plain simple
I treat it with respect
I know it's not perfect
I fuel it with food that serves as energy
This fuel creates a lot of synergy
I respect my boundaries created by me
Boys stay away, my body is not free
I must be loved for a period of time
Before I allow you to be all mine
Love is not about using my body
Love is about caring about somebody
I am not a rag doll to throw in a corner
Because it is my body that I do honor.
My body is sacred it is my lifeline
I demand respect for what is mine
My body, my temple is for only me

Root yourself to launch your biggest desires

Above the Clouds

Above the clouds high in the sky
My life stands still as I fly
My heart sings the song of life out loud
My soul opens up and forgets the how
Quietly I sit here, I am at peace
The sound of nature, of life, I seek
Hearing the engines roar on the plane
I meditate and quiet I shall remain
Allowing my heart to open more
High above the clouds, I will soar

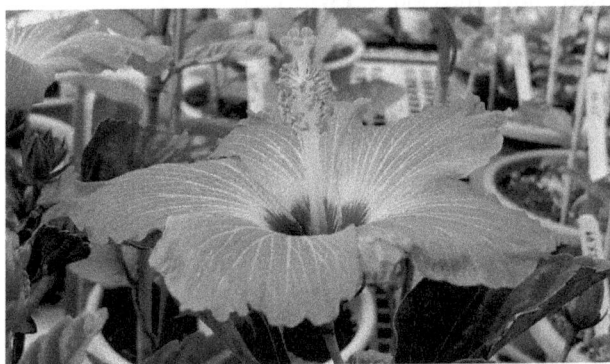

Forever Grateful

Today I am forever grateful
No more worries no need to be hateful
People come into your life when the time is right
It is healing the blind to have perfect sight
It removes the armor I hold to defend
It allows my heart the time to mend
Being grateful puts ideas in motion
No need for any more commotion
Stand proud, stand tall, stand in your power
Allow the light of gold blossom like a flower
Today in the present send gratefulness above
You will see your life fly like a morning dove

Daily affirmation:

I am a strong, confident person who is an unstoppable force for love and compassion. I will take on new opportunities that serve my higher good. My life is full of riches, not only in money but happiness and love. I continue to learn what feeds my soul. I am a force for courage that I can give to others.

Spark Your Rockstar

Spark your Rockstar an angel would say
Play your song loudly, play it all day
Rock out the dreams that you desire
While you are at it, walk on fire
Shake your ass to change your state
Now your life you will create
Stop now and feel the gratitude
This will create an assttitude
Get up each day and meditate
Thoughts in your mind will dissipate
Stay out of your mind and get into your heart
Magic begins its state-of-the-art
Turn up the music and dance around
Make the world today your playground

Carolyn Rim
https://www.sparkyourrockstar.com/

The Red Door

Take a deep breath
Walk down the seven stairs
See the word release on the red door
The red door opens; what do you see
Opportunity awaits as you relax your mind
Imagination and reality all blend together

Create your dream feel them see them
From this day forward this world is yours

Take a ride on a magic carpet in to the universe
Take a color shower to cleanse your soul

Sit in silence and feel your body sizzle
Flood your emotions stack them one by one

Recharge your energy release it to earth
Play like a child let creativeness flow
Smile from the heart to give the love to others

Hug a tree, visit your spirit animal
Smell a flower, and look at the clouds
Nature's pure magic is right there to experience

Raise the vibration plant the seed of love

Be in your beautiful state, find your authentic self

Let the golden bright light fill every cell of your body

Continued on next page...

Let it flow through you from the heavens to the
earth

Take a deep breath and allow the energy to
surge in you
Walk up the seven stairs through the red door

Open your eyes; your world is around you

Carolyn Rim
https://www.sparkyourrockstar.com/99-day-dare.html

I am awesome in all I do and say with wisdom to share in the world

Identify Yourself

What is it that you use to identify yourself?
Is it measured in fortunes and your wealth?
Will it ever be good enough for you to be happy
Or will your emotions continue to be sappy
Your identity is within you, it is your soul
No need for digging yourself an emotional hole
Close your eyes open your heart
For this is when your identity will start
You will see all the good that you bring
When others are around you, their hearts will sing
The universe provides the map to your identity
You will find it in its own entity
There is no need to compare to others
When you do, your soul it smothers
It is okay for your path to have detours
This is where your identity matures
Your identity is just like a fingerprint
Each with its own unique blueprint
Take the time today to identify yourself
For within you is where there is the greatest wealth.

Life on Earth

So many lives lost in such little time
As you see life on earth can stop on a dime
One thing we should remember and cherish
Their souls will never perish
Even though we are selfish and want them to stay
They are in heaven looking our way
When we get sad wishing they were here
In our hearts they will always be near
Whatever pain that they endured
We know now that God has cured

Join your soul with the universe and ground

Parting Ways

As we leave today
There is something I want to say
We have become one
Connected by earth and sun
We are only a thought away
Close your eyes and feel our presence if you may
Strike your drum to your beat
Soon you will feel our heat
It's the heat of our hearts flowing to you
Surrounding you to feel anew
As you sit by the fire at night
Allow your soul to sour its flight

Boomerang

In the midst of every day
What is it that you want to say
Be kind and gentle to those around you
As they may need it more than you
Love with your heart and soul
Stand up, be proud, and be bold
Dare yourself to take the leap
For beyond the hard is riches you reap
Contribute to others to show you care
The riches of happiness are abundantly there
Be careful what energy you send out
It boomerangs back without a doubt
Take the time to show your gratitude
I promise you, it will uplift your mood
To conclude what I have to say to you
Take in each day, as a grand view

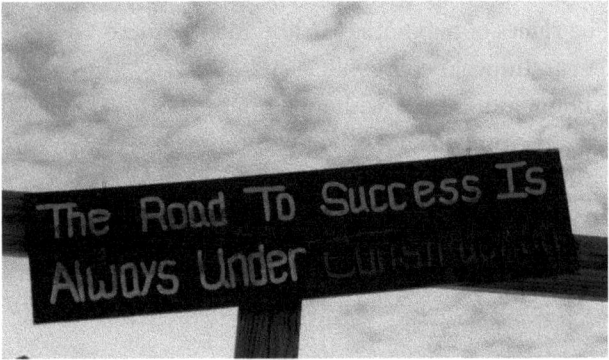

The Road To Success Is Always Under Construction

My soul is telling me to follow my passion and take a leap

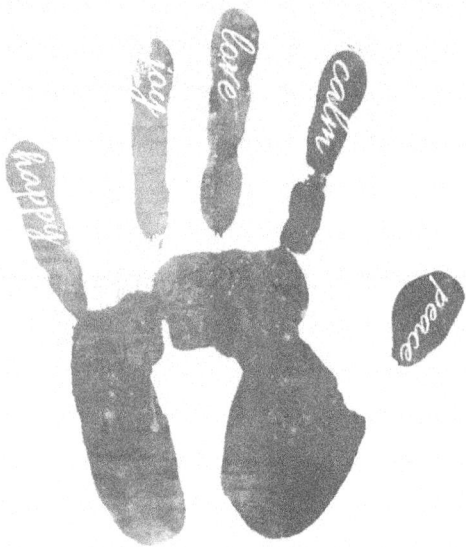

Awesome

Authentically me
Wild dreams created
Enjoying life
Shining my light brightly
Outgoing Personality
Magical
Effervescent

A Mother's Life

A Mother's Life

What does being a mom mean to you?
Are we defined by all that we do
Sitting with your child sick all night
Teaching them how to fly a kite
During the difficult days of a teen
Remember they will think that you are mean
You will do things out of love for them
Even though they are not a perfect gem
Say to yourself *I am strong*
Because you are all day long
I am a force for good for the family
Your wins will show finally
Being a mom is not always easy
Allow yourself to be a little cheesy
Take their words in stride
Just remember they are always your pride
Always leave the door open for a safe place
One day that may be their saving grace
Being a mom is a treasure
Her love can never be measured

Changing Seasons

Living in the Midwest we have a change of seasons
For this, you will love them for many reasons.
In the spring, all things become new
The rain is fresh just as the morning dew
Summer is full of color and light
Oh my, it's a beautiful sight
During the fall, nature winds down
The colors, they turn yellow orange and brown
Now you have winter, the snow so white
It is time to have that snowball fight.
The changing seasons are such a beauty to see
Just thinking about it will create chi

Ask yourself; is it a reaction or a response?

Traveling Afar

What is it your after when you travel afar
Is it the moments you collect and put in a jar
Where we live is just a pin in the haystack
There is more around you, so much to keep track
The earth it has so many wonders to see
Places that I know that I yearn to be
Untouched land people never think of
Souls soaring and sharing the love
Take a look around and tell me what is there
I am alive! My heart is open is what I declare
Slow down, take a moment and take in the view
This is where your soul charges and life is anew

Once Upon a Choice

Once upon a choice I have decided it can be easy

It can be easy to take control of my feelings

It can be easy to live in pure joy and happiness

It can be easy to send love

It can be easy to write my story

It can be easy

I am love and have abundance of it to share

That Guy's House

In That Guy's House what do you learn
It is being real and taking that turn
Building friendships that last a lifetime
Making time stand still, stopping on a dime
Creating from your soul a mandala
Or attending a magical gala
Doing the work that makes you feel uncomfortable
Will bring your soul to a new level
Shifting from a place of chance to a place of choice
Your soul will begin to rejoice
Learning to respond instead of react
Will empower you so, to be exact
Allowing your heart to sing its song
Writing away all day long
Discovering now that instead of a writer
You have transformed into an author

Be True to You

What does it mean to be true to you?
Is it going through life on automatic play?
Is it following the beliefs you have carried the
year through?
Or is it being authentic in all your ways
Does it mean to you to put others happiness first?
Or believe that you are important and need to
take care of you

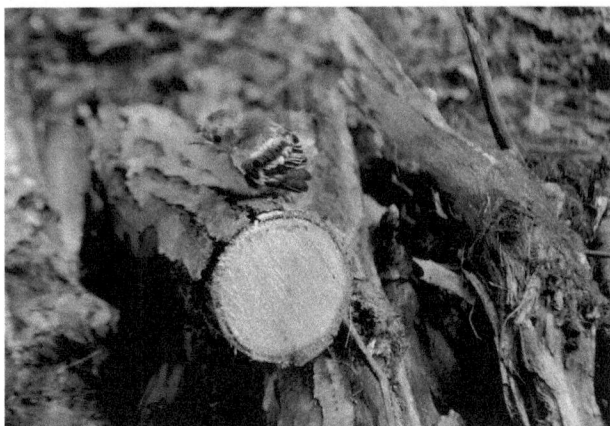

Just remember, whatever life dilemmas your child has, it does not mean it belongs to you

Please Don't Go

When you are miles away from me
There is so much I wish that could be
I wish for you my daughter

To put in your life more laughter
I want to take your pain away
It is happiness that I want you to experience today
I know that the days can be dark and scary
When they are, think of unicorns and fairies

Place your hand on your heart and feel it beat
That is giving you life which is grand and complete
Look up to the stars in the sky above
To find in you all the love

When you love yourself with no conditions attached
You will see infinite possibilities that begin to hatch
As you lay down your head tonight and sleep
Imagine yourself taking the new leap

The leap into the life of your dreams
Where everything is possible just as it seems.
So now that you are here and possibilities you see
Take your momma's hand and take a walk in
complete glee

Your momma loves you more than anyone ever will
Feel that love in you, feel it build and be still

Continued on next page...

My little one, I promise everything will be okay

Those hurtful feelings will begin to fade away
I promise that I will be by your side every step you take
I will walk by you and support you through
any heartache

Love,

Your Momma

MY DAUGHTER

My Daughter

My daughter is a beautiful bright soul
Who has many gifts to offer the world.
She is processing her emotions
And will figure it out.

THE END

The Purpose of life is to live it.

Meet Dana Zimmerman

Dana is a bright soul who has found her awesomeness in life through experiences that at first weighed her down. She has come from a bottomless pit of despair and made her way through by strength through friends and healing by learning.

Through poetry, she learned that sometimes you need to be broken to find the beauty in the moment. These are expressed in the poems written.

The life experiences here are formed by life events from abuse, separation, mental illness, times of joy and peace. The moment captured explains the emotion going on and moving through it.

The pictures were captured that gives symbol to the moment to give you a visual to feel it. This path for her has been hard work. However, she recently came to the realization, "It Can Be Easy!"

Photo Credits

Also by That Guy's House

Finding Lilly by Elizabeth Goddard

www.ingramcontent.com/pod-product-compliance
Lightning Source LLC
Chambersburg PA
CBHW071550040426
42452CB00008B/1130